MW00442109

FingerTips
WITH
A TOUCH OF THEORY

A TECHNIQUE AND THEORY WORKBOOK FOR PIANO

By Elizabeth D. Cobb

Jane S. Lewis

Judith R. Strickland

Edited by

Victoria McArthur

CONTENTS

Production: Frank and Gail Hackinson

Production Coordination, Cover and
Text Design: Marilyn Cole

Editors: Victoria McArthur and
Edwin McLean

Engraving: GrayBear Music Company,
Hollywood, Florida

Printer: Trend Graphics

PRACTICE PLAN FOR BOOK 1

Teacher's Note:

This practice plan provides a structure for practicing the keyboard skills presented in Book 1.
It is intended to be transposed to other keys as they are introduced.

I. Major Pentascale, parallel and contrary.

II. Major Triad, parallel and contrary.

III. Minor Pentascale, parallel and contrary.

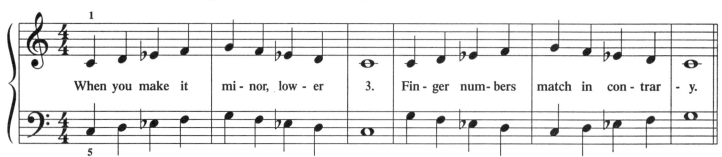

IV. Minor Triad, parallel and contrary.

C Major Pentascale

The C MAJOR PENTASCALE uses the notes **C D E F G.**

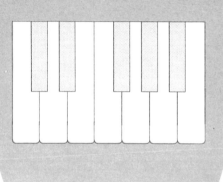

C Major Pentascale

1. Write the letter names on the keyboard below.

The pattern of whole and half steps in all major pentascales is whole, whole, half, whole.

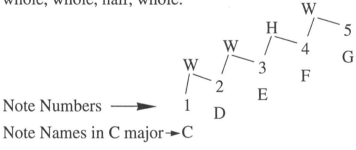

Note Numbers →

Note Names in C major → C

2. CHECK (✔) the white keys below that form a half step in the C major pentascale.
Then WRITE the letter names on the (✔) keys.

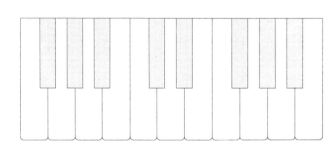

---

3. WRITE C major pentascales in both treble and bass clef.
CIRCLE the notes a half step apart.

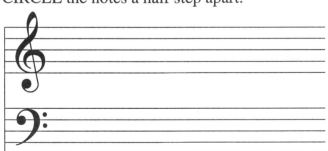

4. FILL IN the blanks below.

In major pentascales the half step is between note numbers ___ and ___.

5. To learn the pentascale finger numbers, PLAY in the air the finger numbers below.
PLAY hands separately, then hands together.

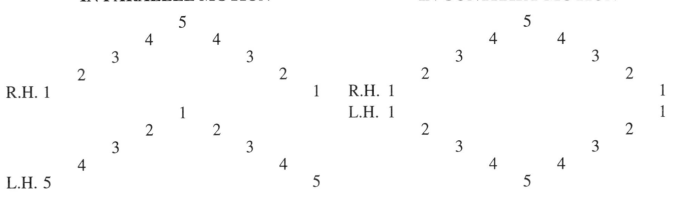

IN PARALLEL MOTION

IN CONTRARY MOTION

Practice Plan for Major Pentascales

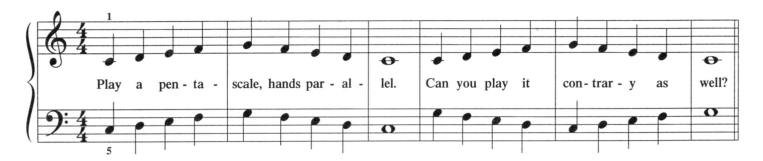

Play a pen-ta-scale, hands par-al-lel. Can you play it con-trar-y as well?

6. Using the Practice Plan above with the C major pentascale

- PLAY hands separately, then hands together when you are ready.
- PLAY *forte* (loud) with firm fingertips, then PLAY *piano* (soft) also with firm fingertips.
- SING or SAY the words as you PLAY.

7. COMPLETE the crossword below.

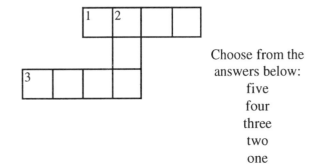

Choose from the
answers below:
five
four
three
two
one

ACROSS
1. The half step in a major pentascale
   is between notes three and _____ .

3. How many notes in a pentascale? _____

DOWN
2. How many half steps in a pentascale? _____

G Major Pentascale

The G MAJOR PENTASCALE
uses the notes **G A B C D.**

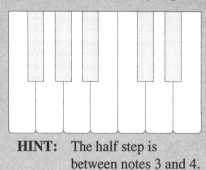

G Major Pentascale

1. Write the letter names on the keyboard below.
   Then CHECK (✔) the white keys below that
   form a half step in the G major pentascale.

   HINT: The half step is
   between notes 3 and 4.

2. **Using the G major pentascale, follow the Practice Plan on page 4.**

   - PLAY pentascales with good hand position.
   - PLAY with correct fingers every time.
   - Always PLAY with a steady rhythm.

3. WRITE G major pentascales in both treble and bass clef.
   CIRCLE the notes a half step apart.

FingerTip

*"Playing the piano with
long fingernails is like
walking on ice skates."*

4. CIRCLE the correct answers for the examples below.

   a.   contrary motion
        parallel motion

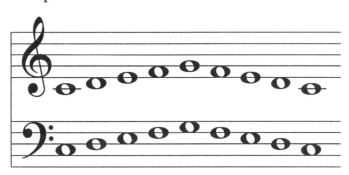

   b.   contrary motion
        parallel motion

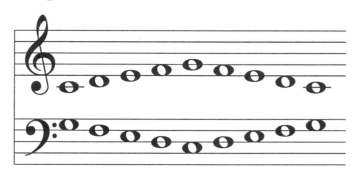

   c.   In parallel motion,
        your hands move in the *opposite* direction.
                         TRUE or FALSE
                         (circle one)

   d.   In *parallel* motion,
        use the same finger numbers in both hands.
                         TRUE or FALSE
                         (circle one)

---

5. CIRCLE the notes a half step apart in the pentascale below.

---

6. Finger Warm-ups for Pentascales

PLAY the finger patterns using the C major pentascale hands separately, then hands together.
Repeat using the G major pentascale.

   a.   R.H.
           1 2   1 2   1 2   1
       L.H.   *fermata*   ⌢   means hold the note longer.

   b.   R.H.
           2 3   2 3   2 3   2
       L.H.   *repeat sign*   :‖   means repeat the section.

   c.   R.H.
           3 4   3 4   3 4   3
       L.H.

C and G Minor Pentascales

Change the major pentascale to minor
by lowering the third note one half step.

The C MINOR PENTASCALE
uses the notes **C D E♭ F G.**

C Minor Pentascale

1. WRITE the letter names on the keyboard below.

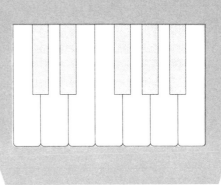

The pattern of whole and half steps
in the minor pentascale
is whole, half, whole, whole.

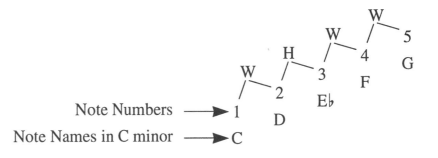

Note Numbers ⟶ 1
Note Names in C minor ⟶ C

2. FILL IN the blanks below.

In minor pentascales the half step
is between note numbers ____ and ____.

Practice Plan for Minor Pentascales

When you make it mi - nor, low - er 3. Fin - ger num - bers match in con - trar - y.

3. **Using the Practice Plan above with the C minor pentascale**

- PLAY hands separately, then hands together when you are ready.
- SING or SAY the words as you play.

The G MINOR PENTASCALE uses the notes **G A B♭ C D.**

G Minor Pentascale

4. WRITE the letter names on the keyboard below. Then CHECK the keys that form a half step.

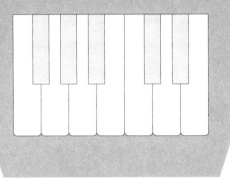

5. Now **PLAY the Practice Plan on page 7 using the G minor pentascale.**

6. WRITE C and G minor pentascales in both treble and bass clef. Then CIRCLE the notes that form half steps.

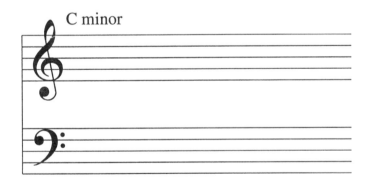

C minor

G minor

7. COMPLETE the crossword below.

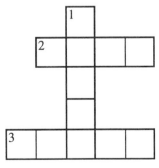

ACROSS

2. A flat (♭) makes a note go _____ (**up or down**)?

3. The half step in a minor pentascale is between notes two and _____ (**one or three**)?

DOWN

1. A flat (♭) makes a note a half step _____ (**higher or lower**)?

LESSON 4

C and G Major Triads

The C MAJOR TRIAD is built from the 1st, 3rd, and 5th notes of a C MAJOR PENTASCALE.
The notes are **C E G.** Another name for a triad is chord.

A triad may be played **blocked** (all notes at once), or **broken** (one note at a time).

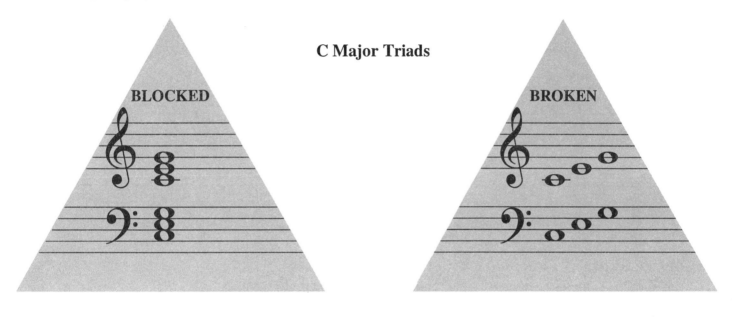

C Major Triads

BLOCKED   BROKEN

---

1. CIRCLE the pentascale note numbers
   that form a triad below.

   1 2 3 4 5

2. CIRCLE the letters used
   for the C major triad below.

   A B C D E F G A B C

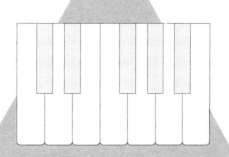

4. WRITE the letter names of the
   C major triad on the keyboard above.

3. **Brain Teasers**
   FILL IN the blanks.

   A tricycle has _____ wheels.
   A triangle has _____ sides.
   A triad has _____ notes.

5. To learn the triad finger patterns, PLAY in the air the finger numbers below
hands separately, then hands together.

BLOCKED

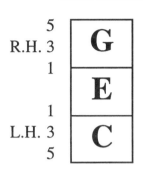

BROKEN

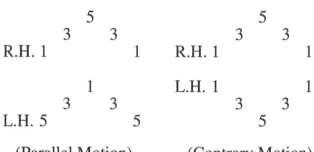

(Parallel Motion)   (Contrary Motion)

Practice Plan for Major Triads

Please play it par - al - lel. Con - trar - y now as well.

6. Using the Practice Plan above with the C major triad
- PLAY hands separately, then hands together when you are ready.
- SING or SAY the words as you PLAY blocked and broken triads.

Remember . . .

- *Keep wrists and arms relaxed.*
- *Play on firm, curved fingertips.*
- *Use fingers 1, 3, 5 every time.*
- *Listen for even tones.*

---

7. COMPLETE the crossword below.

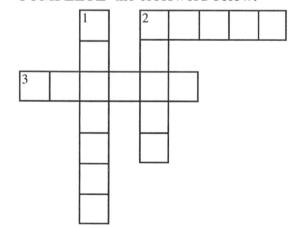

CHOOSE from these answers:

blocked,   broken,   steps,   skips

ACROSS
2. A triad is made up of _____.
3. A _____ triad means to play notes one at a time.

DOWN
1. A _____ triad means to play notes together.
2. A pentascale is made up of _____.

8. Now PLAY the Practice Plan on page 10 with the G major triad.
The G MAJOR TRIAD uses the notes **G B D.**

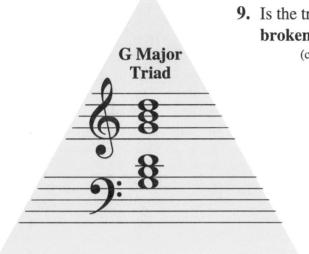

9. Is the triad to the left
broken or **blocked**?
(circle one)

10. WRITE the letter names of the
G major triad on the keyboard above.

---

11. WRITE on each staff below:

C Major Blocked Triad

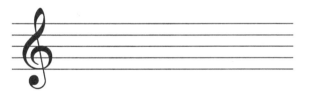

G Major Blocked Triad

C Major Broken Triad

G Major Broken Triad

---

12. Finger Warm-ups for Major Triads
PLAY both hands separately, then together. Repeat using the G major triad.
(Left hand plays one octave lower than written.)

a.

b.

c.

LESSON 5

C and G Minor Triads

The C MINOR TRIAD uses the 1st, 3rd, and 5th notes of a C MINOR PENTASCALE.
Another way to find a minor triad is to lower the 3rd of a major triad one half step.
The notes are **C E♭ G.**

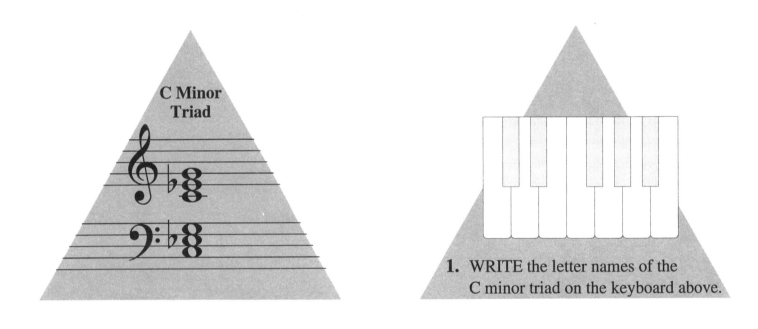

1. WRITE the letter names of the C minor triad on the keyboard above.

Practice Plan for Minor Triads

Change to a mi - nor key. Now play it con - trar - y.

2. **Using the Practice Plan above with the C minor triad**
   - PLAY hands separately, then hands together when you are ready.
   - SING or SAY the words as you PLAY.

FF106

The G Minor Triad

PLAY the G major triad.
Now change it to G minor by lowering the 3rd one half step.

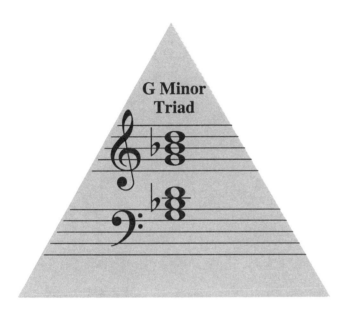

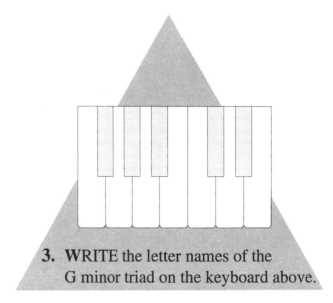

3. WRITE the letter names of the G minor triad on the keyboard above.

4. **PLAY the Practice Plan with the G minor triad.**
   Remember . . .

    "When you make it minor, lower 3."

5. WRITE minor triads in both clefs as indicated below.

| G Minor Triad | | C Minor Triad | |
| Blocked | Broken | Blocked | Broken |

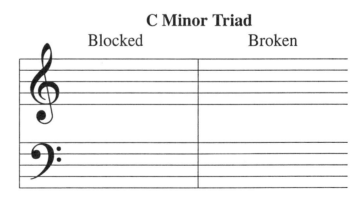

6. **Combine the Practice Plans for major and minor pentascales and triads.**

   PLAY the Practice Plan on page 2 in this order:
   - C major, C minor
   - G major, G minor

F Major and Minor Pentascales and Triads

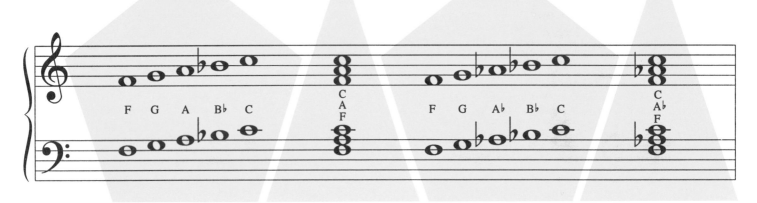

F Major Pentascale   **F Major Triad**   **F Minor Pentascale**   **F Minor Triad**

1. WRITE letter names for the pentascales and triads on the keyboards below.

F Major Pentascale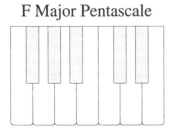

F Major Triad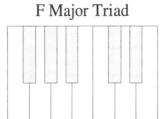

F Minor Pentascale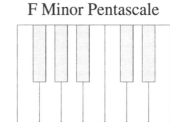

F Minor Triad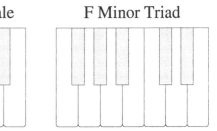

2. WRITE on each staff below:

F Major Pentascale

F Minor Pentascale

F Major Triad

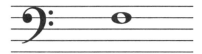

F Minor Triad

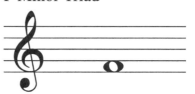

3. **PLAY the Practice Plan on page 2 for pentascales and triads in F major and F minor.**
PLAY hands separately, then together.

FingerTip
"Play on the tips of your fingers."

---

4. CIRCLE **a** or **b** below.

How are C, G, and F major triads alike?
    a. all white keys
    b. black key in the middle

How are C, G, and F minor triads alike?
    a. all white keys
    b. black key in the middle

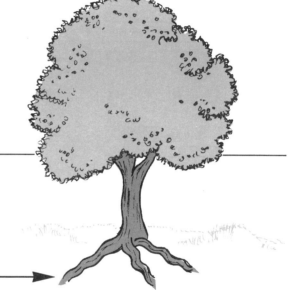

The **ROOT** of a triad ──────▶
is the note on which a triad is built.
For example, C is the ROOT of a C triad.

5. FILL IN the blanks below.

The ROOT of the G triad is _____.

The ROOT of the F triad is _____.

---

6. **Finger Warm-ups for Minor Triads**
PLAY both hands separately, then together.
Then also play the warm-ups in C and G positions.
(L.H. plays one octave lower than written.)

a.

b.

D Major and Minor Pentascales and Triads

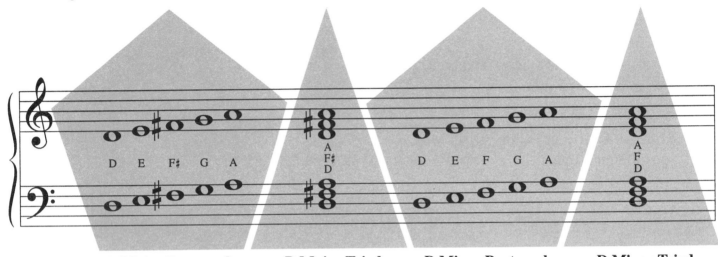

D Major Pentascale   D Major Triad   D Minor Pentascale   D Minor Triad

1. WRITE letter names for the pentascales and triads on the keyboards below.

D Major Pentascale   D Major Triad   D Minor Pentascale   D Minor Triad

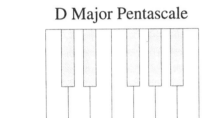 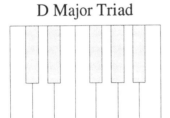 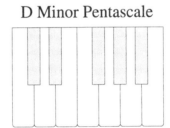 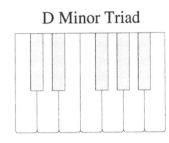

2. WRITE the **fingering** for the D broken triads below the notes.

 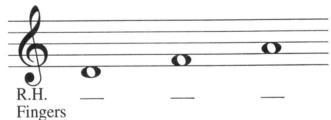

L.H. Fingers   ___   ___   ___   R.H. Fingers   ___   ___   ___

3. CHECK (✔) the black key used in the D major triad.
   Then WRITE the name on that key.

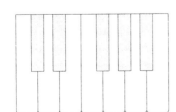

4. WRITE a D major triad on the staff below.

5. COMPLETE the crossword below.

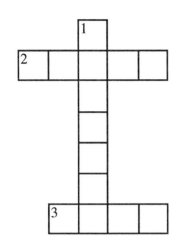

CHOOSE from these answers:
    natural
    flat
    sharp

ACROSS

    2. ♯ is called a _____ sign.

    3. ♭ is called a _____ sign.

DOWN

    1. ♮ is called a _____ sign.

---

6. WRITE the D major pentascale in contrary motion.

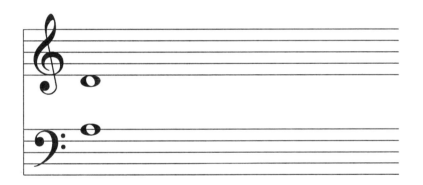

FingerTip

"Playing without curved fingers is like walking stiff-legged."

---

7. PLAY the Practice Plan for the pentascales and triads in D major and minor.
(Refer to page 2, if needed)

REVIEW the Practice Plan for pentascales and triads in C, G, and F major and minor.

Try to vary your practice daily by:
- Playing one hand *staccato,* the other hand *legato.*   **Staccato** means detached.
  Legato means connected.

- Playing one hand *forte,* the other hand *piano.*   **Forte** (*f*) means loud.
  Piano (*p*) means soft.

The Practice Plan can be played in 20 seconds in each key.

A Major and Minor Pentascales and Triads

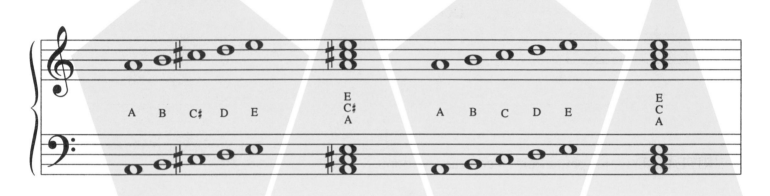

A Major Pentascale   **A Major Triad**   **A Minor Pentascale**   **A Minor Triad**

1. WRITE letter names for the pentascales and triads on the keyboards below.

A Major Pentascale | A Major Triad | A Minor Pentascale | A Minor Triad

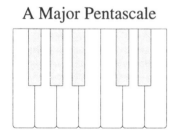 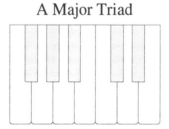 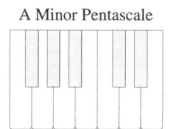 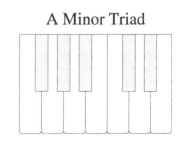

2. Using the melody below, CIRCLE T (true) or F (false) for each question.

   a. Measure 1 has a broken triad going up.   (T or F)
   b. Measure 2 has a pentascale going up.   (T or F)
   c. The triad and pentascale are major.   (T or F)
   d. The melody has a G minor broken triad. (T or F)

   A dot (·) over or under a note means to play it *staccato*.

3. PLAY the melody above as written, then again starting on C, F, and D.

   Playing the same pattern starting on a different note is called **transposing**.

4. CIRCLE **a** or **b** below.

How are the D and A major pentascales alike?
- a. all white keys
- b. black key in the middle

How are the D and A minor pentascales alike?
- a. all white keys
- b. black key in the middle

---

5. CHECK (✔) the black key used in the A major triad.
Then WRITE the name on that key.

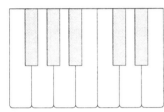

6. WRITE an A major triad on the staff below.

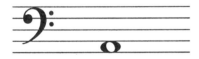

---

7. WRITE A minor pentascales in parallel motion using both clefs below.

---

8. PLAY the Practice Plan in A major and minor.

REVIEW by PLAYING the Practice Plan for pentascales and triads in C, G, F, and D major and minor.

Try to vary your practice daily by:
- Playing both hands *mezzo forte* (*mf*), then *mezzo piano* (*mp*).   *mf* means moderately loud.
  mp means moderately soft.
- Playing a *crescendo* (——◁) for the entire example.   *Crescendo* means to play gradually louder.

E Major and Minor Pentascales and Triads

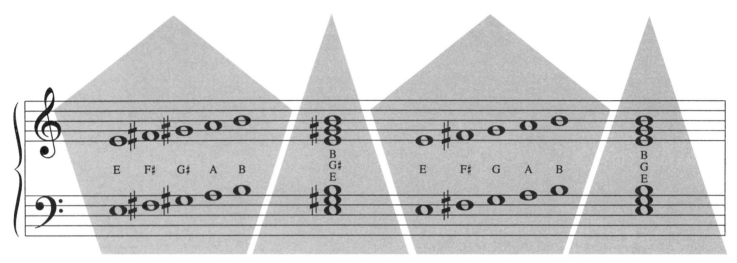

E Major Pentascale   **E Major Triad**   **E Minor Pentascale**   **E Minor Triad**

1. WRITE letter names for the pentascales and triads on the keyboards below.

E Major Pentascale   E Major Triad   E Minor Pentascale   E Minor Triad

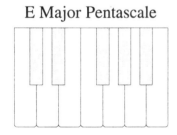 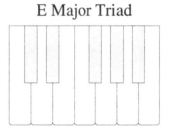 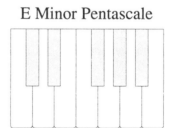 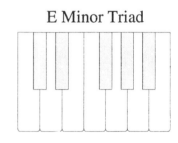

2. **Using the Practice Plan with E major and minor**
   PLAY each hand separately, then together when you are ready.

3. DRAW lines to connect signs to the English and Italian terms.

ENGLISH TERM	SIGN	ITALIAN TERM
Ex. loud	*p*	mezzo forte
soft	*mp*	forte
moderately loud	*f*	piano
moderately soft	*mf*	mezzo piano

4. CIRCLE the letter names for the WHITE KEY TRIADS below:

Ex. C Major	A	B	Ⓒ	D	Ⓔ	F	Ⓖ	A	B
G Major	C	D	E	F	G	A	B	C	D
F Major	E	F	G	A	B	C	D	E	F
A Minor	G	A	B	C	D	E	F	G	A
E Minor	B	C	D	E	F	G	A	B	C
D Minor	D	E	F	G	A	B	C	D	E

5. WRITE the letter names for the triad notes on the keyboards below.

D Major Triad

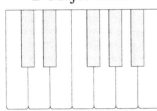

E Major Triad

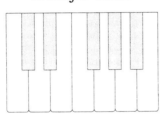

A Major Triad

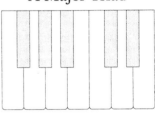

6. FILL IN **a**, **b**, or **c** to answer the questions below.

The key colors are:
a. white - black - white.
b. black - white - white.
c. white - white - white.

How are the three triads above (D, E, A) alike? _____

How are the major triads alike when changed to minor? _____

7. WRITE on each staff below:

E Major Pentascale

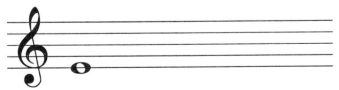

E Minor Pentascale

E Major Triad, Blocked and Broken

E Minor Triad, Blocked and Broken

LESSON 10

E Flat (♭) Major and Minor Pentascales and Triads

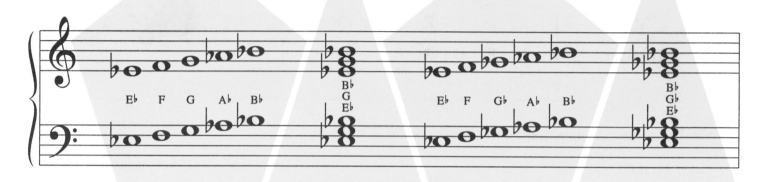

E♭ Major Pentascale   E♭ Major Triad   E♭ Minor Pentascale   E♭ Minor Triad

1. WRITE letter names for the pentascales and triads on the keyboards below.

E♭ Major Pentascale   E♭ Major Triad   E♭ Minor Pentascale   E♭ Minor Triad

2. Now follow the Practice Plan with E♭ major and minor.
PLAY hands separately, then togeth

3. ANSWER the questions below.

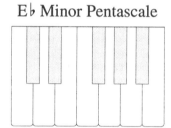

In a major
pentascale, the
half step is between the
_____ and _____ notes.
In a minor pentascale, the half step is
between the _____ and _____ notes.
Are the patterns below M (major) or m (minor)?

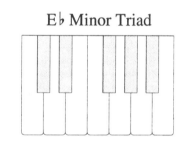

1 ⌃2 ⌃3 ⌃4 ⌃5   =   M or m?
W   W   H   W   (circle one)

1 ⌃2 ⌃3 ⌃4 ⌃5   =   M or m?
W   H   W   W   (circle one)

FingerTip

*"Try not to twist your hand
as you play the black keys."*

22

4. DRAW a line from the **Keyboard Skill** to the **Melody** that uses it, then from the **Melody** to the **Melody Name.**

Keyboard Skill	**Melody**	**Melody Name**

(Teacher may wish to play for the student.)

F Major Pentascale — The First Noël

D Major Pentascale — Jingle Bells

Broken C Major Triad — God Rest You Merry, Gentlemen

E Minor Pentascale — Deck the Halls

5. WRITE the letter names for the E and E♭ major pentascales on the keyboards to the right.

FILL IN the blanks below.

The **black** keys in the E major pentascale are _____ _____.

The **white** keys in the E♭ major pentascale are _____ _____.

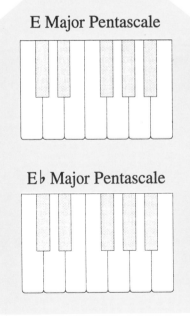

E Major Pentascale

E♭ Major Pentascale

23

LESSON 11

A Flat (♭) Major and Minor Pentascales and Triads

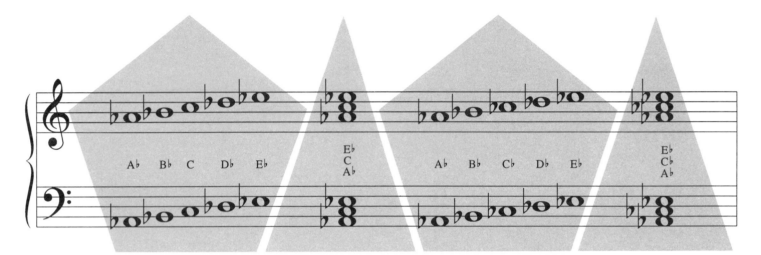

A♭ Major Pentascale **A♭ Major Triad** **A♭ Minor Pentascale** **A♭ Minor Triad**

1. WRITE letter names for the pentascales and triads on the keyboards below.

A♭ Major Pentascale

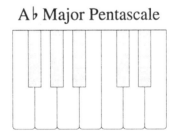

A♭ Major Triad

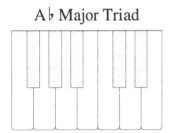

A♭ Minor Pentascale

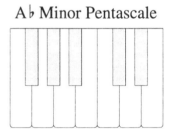

A♭ Minor Triad

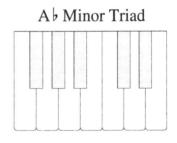

2. **Using the Practice Plan in the keys of A♭ major and minor**
   PLAY hands separately, then hands together when you are ready.

3. WRITE the pentascales and triads below.
   WATCH for the clef changes.

A♭ Major Pentascale   A♭ Major Triad   A♭ Minor Pentascale   A♭ Minor Triad

FF1064

4. Many keys can have two names.

Can you FILL IN the blanks below
with a second name for these keys?

Another name for D♭ is _____.

Another name for E♭ is _____.

Another name for F is _____.

Another name for G♭ is _____.

Another name for A♭ is _____.

---

5. WRITE the letter names for the A and A♭ major
pentascales on the keyboards to the right.

FILL IN the blanks below.

The only **black** key in the
A major triad is _____.

The only **white** key in the
A♭ major triad is _____.

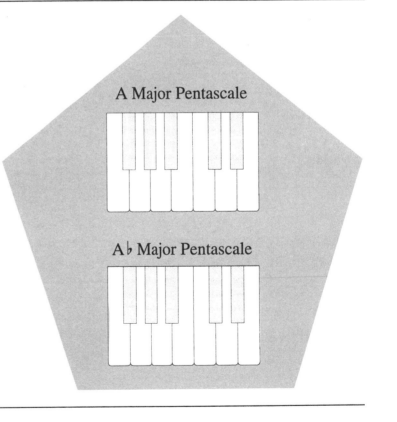

A Major Pentascale

A♭ Major Pentascale

---

6. **COMPARE the pentascales and triads in the keys of E and E♭ major and minor
as you PLAY the Practice Plan .**

- Then REVIEW the Practice Plan for pentascales and triads
  in C, G, F, D, and A major and minor.

- For a challenge, try PLAYING with the metronome set at ♩ = 120.

LESSON 12

D Flat (♭) Major and Minor Pentascales and Triads

C Sharp (♯) Major and Minor Pentascales and Triads

D♭ Major Pentascale   D♭ Major Triad   D♭ Minor Pentascale   D♭ Minor Triad

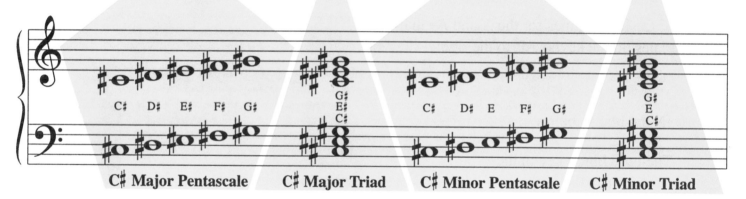

C♯ Major Pentascale   C♯ Major Triad   C♯ Minor Pentascale   C♯ Minor Triad

The word **enharmonic** means another name for the same sound.
For example, D♭ and C♯ are different notes that sound the same.

---

1. WRITE the letter names for the pentascales and triads on the keyboards below.

D♭ Major Pentascale   D♭ Major Triad   D♭ Minor Pentascale   D♭ Minor Triad

C♯ Major Pentascale   C♯ Major Triad   C♯ Minor Pentascale   C♯ Minor Triad

26

2. Using the Practice Plans for D♭ and C♯ major and minor

- PLAY the D♭ major and minor pentascales, hands separately.
- PLAY the C♯ major and minor pentascales, hands together.

---

3. COMPARE the D♭ and C♯ major pentascales after WRITING the letter names on the keyboards to the right.

ANSWER the questions below.

What is the only white key in D♭? _____

What is the only white key in C♯? _____

How are D♭ and C♯ major pentascales alike? _____

The enharmonic name for C♯ is _____.

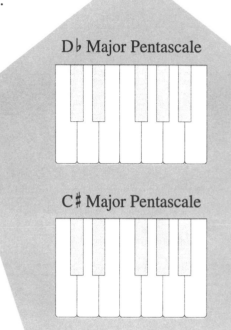

D♭ Major Pentascale

C♯ Major Pentascale

---

4. WRITE the D♭ major pentascale and triad below.

D♭ Major Pentascale   D♭ Major Triad

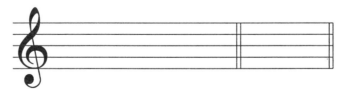

5. WRITE the C♯ minor pentascale and triad below.

C♯ Minor Pentascale   C♯ Minor Triad

6. WRITE the answers to the questions below.

What note is flatted but played on a white key in D♭ minor? _____

What note is flatted but played on a white key in A♭ minor? _____.

27

B Major and Minor Pentascales and Triads
C Flat (♭) Major Pentascale and Triad

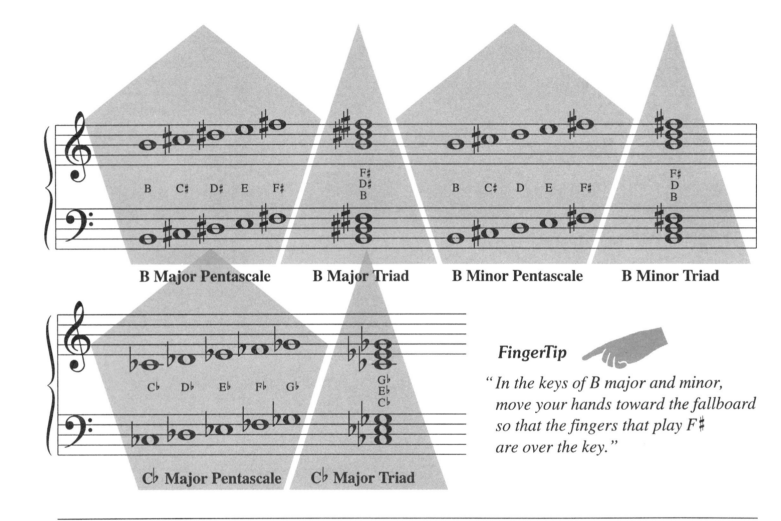

B Major Pentascale   B Major Triad   B Minor Pentascale   B Minor Triad

C♭ Major Pentascale   C♭ Major Triad

FingerTip

" *In the keys of B major and minor, move your hands toward the fallboard so that the fingers that play F♯ are over the key.*"

1. WRITE the letter names for the pentascales and triads on the keyboards below.

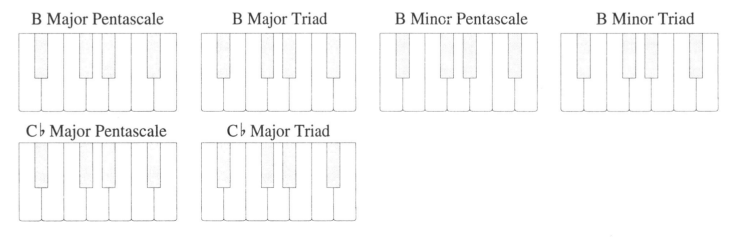

B Major Pentascale   B Major Triad   B Minor Pentascale   B Minor Triad

C♭ Major Pentascale   C♭ Major Triad

2. Now PLAY the Practice Plan in B major and minor, and C♭ major.

PLAY hands separately, then together when you are ready.

---

3. DRAW a line to connect the **Sign** to its matching **Term,**
then from the **Term** to its **Meaning.**

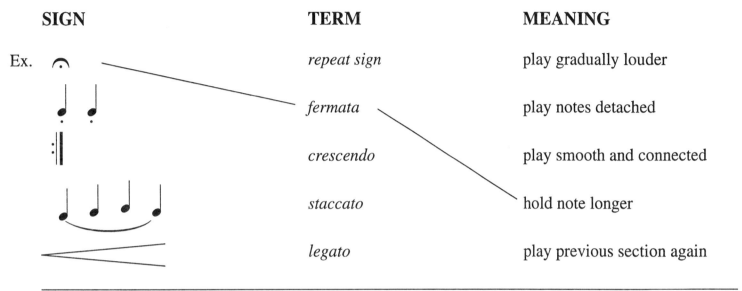

SIGN	TERM	MEANING
Ex.	repeat sign	play gradually louder
	fermata	play notes detached
	crescendo	play smooth and connected
	staccato	hold note longer
	legato	play previous section again

---

4. Using the Practice Plans for B major and minor, and C♭ major

- PLAY the B major and minor pentascales hands separately.
- PLAY the C♭ major pentascale hands together.

---

5. WRITE the B and C♭ major pentascales
on the keyboards to the right.

ANSWER the questions below.

What is the enharmonic name for E? _____

What is the enharmonic name for C♯? _____

What are the notes in the C♭ major triad?

_____ _____ _____

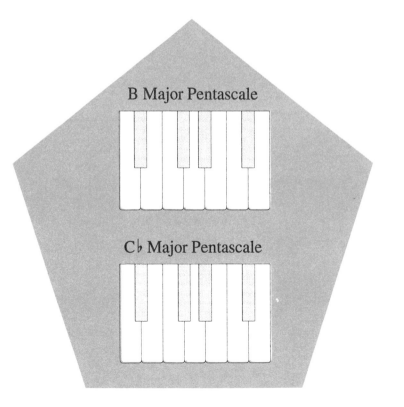

B Major Pentascale

C♭ Major Pentascale

F Sharp (♯) Major and Minor Pentascales and Triads

G Flat (♭) Major Pentascale and Triad

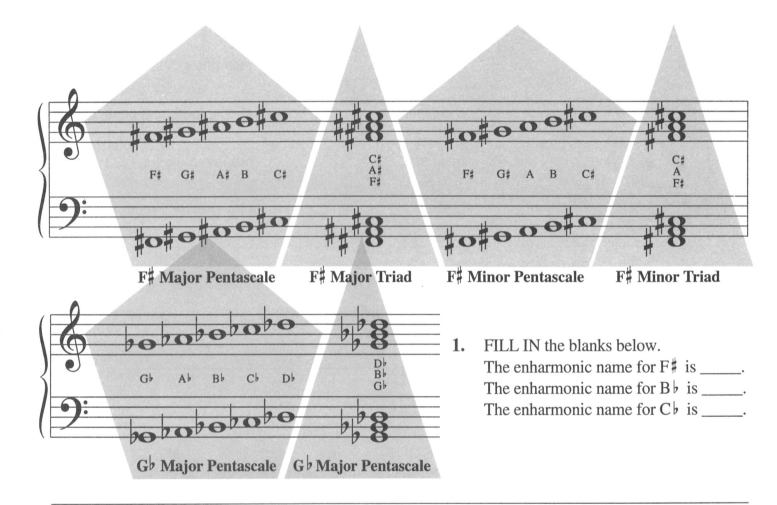

F♯ Major Pentascale   F♯ Major Triad   F♯ Minor Pentascale   F♯ Minor Triad

G♭ Major Pentascale   G♭ Major Pentascale

1. FILL IN the blanks below.
   The enharmonic name for F♯ is _____.
   The enharmonic name for B♭ is _____.
   The enharmonic name for C♭ is _____.

2. WRITE the letter names for the pentascales and triads on the keyboards below.

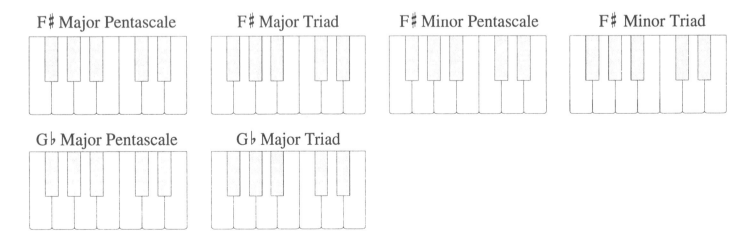

F♯ Major Pentascale   F♯ Major Triad   F♯ Minor Pentascale   F♯ Minor Triad

G♭ Major Pentascale   G♭ Major Triad

3. WRITE the pentascales and triads below.

G♭ Major Pentascale

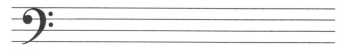

F♯ Major Pentascale

F♯ Minor Pentascale

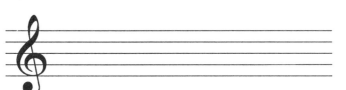

G♭ Major Triad   F♯ Major Triad

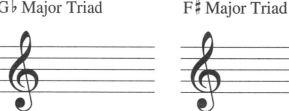

---

4. **Now follow the Practice Plan with F♯ major and minor, and G♭ major.**

Hints for Practicing

Make practicing more fun by varying it daily. Try one or two of these suggestions each day.

a. Play the major pentascales and triads you have learned in this order:
   C, G, F,   D, A, E,   D♭, A♭, E♭,   G♭ (F♯)

b. Play the pentascales and triads that you have learned, beginning with C, and moving up by half steps.

c. Play the minor pentascales and triads, hands together in parallel motion.

d. Play the major and minor pentascales, hands together in contrary motion.

e. Play the major and minor triads broken.

f. Play the major pentascales and triads, hands together with dynamics of your choice.

g. Play the minor pentascales and triads, hands separately staccato.

h. Make up your own rhythm as you play the pentascales.

Remember . . .
   - *Always listen to your playing.*
   - *Always play with a clear, beautiful sound.*
   - *Always play with a good, rounded hand position.*

B Flat (♭) Major and Minor Pentascales and Triads

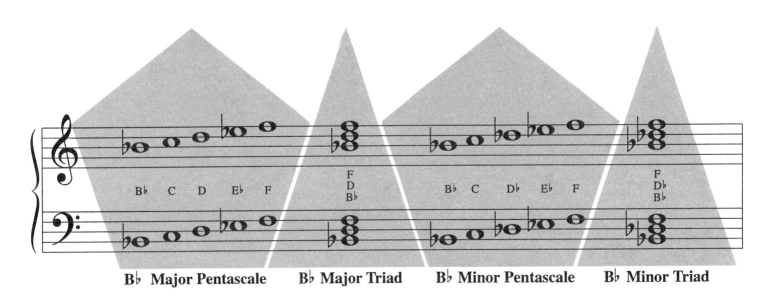

B♭ Major Pentascale   B♭ Major Triad   B♭ Minor Pentascale   B♭ Minor Triad

1. WRITE the letter names for the pentascales and triads on the keyboards below.

B♭ Major Pentascale   B♭ Major Triad   B♭ Minor Pentascale   B♭ Minor Triad

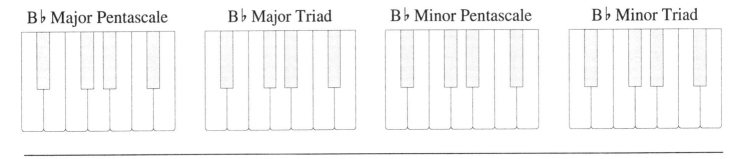

2. DRAW a line from the **Keyboard Skill** to the **Melody** that uses it,
then from the **Melody** to the **Melody Name.**

Keyboard Skill   **Melody**   **Melody Name**
(Teacher may wish to play for the student.)

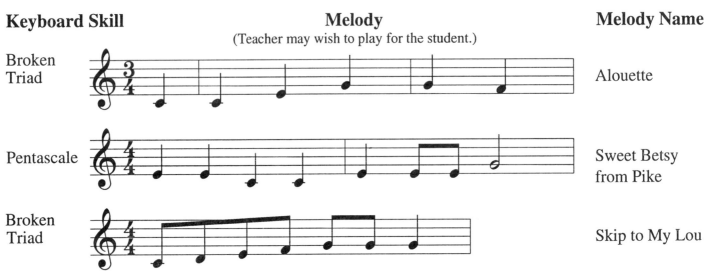

Broken Triad   Alouette

Pentascale   Sweet Betsy from Pike

Broken Triad   Skip to My Lou

3. Using the Practice Plan with pentascales and triads in B♭ major and minor

PLAY hands separately, then together when you are ready.

_____

4. WRITE the pentascales and triads below.
COMPARE the triads in B and B♭ major. How are they different? _____

B Major Pentascale

B Major Triad

B♭ Major Pentascale

B♭ Major Triad

5. Keyboard Quiz

Answer the questions by PLAYING first, then WRITING the answer.

a. How are C, G, and F major triads alike?   _____

b. Which major pentascale is slightly different from the other two?   C   G   F   (circle)

c. How are D, A, and E minor triads alike?   _____

d. How are D and D♭ major pentascales different?   _____

e. Which major triad does not belong in this group?   D♭   A♭   G♭   E♭   (circle)

f. How are G♭ major and F♯ major pentascales alike?   _____

6. REVIEW by PLAYING the Practice Plan in all keys.

The Practice Plan in all keys can be played in only 8 minutes!

Matching Game

DRAW lines connecting the **Musical Example** to the **Term.**

Musical Example   **Term**

   pentascale

   root of the D♭ triad

   finger patterns in contrary motion

   whole step

   broken major triad

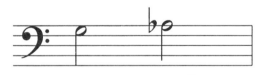   finger patterns in parallel motion

```
                5
          4         4
       3              3
    2                    2
R.H. 1                      1
L.H. 1  2                 2  1
          3            3
             4      4
                5
```
                                                          half step

```
                5
          4         4
       3              3
    2                    2
R.H. 1         1            1
          3  2   2  3
             4      4
L.H. 5                      5
```
                                                          blocked minor triad

TERMS AND DEFINITIONS

accidentals .... sharps, flats, and naturals not found in the key signature

blocked triad or chord ...... a chord with the notes played together

broken triad or chord .... a chord with the notes played one at a time

chord .... three or more notes played together blocked or broken

contrary motion .... opposite movement in which one part goes up as another goes down

crescendo .... to play gradually louder ($\textstyle\fbox{}$)

dynamics .... words or symbols that indicate how loud or soft to play

enharmonic .... notes that sound the same but are written differently

fermata .... the symbol meaning to pause or hold longer ($\frown$)

flat .... the symbol that lowers a note a half step ($\flat$)

forte .... loud (f)

half step .... the distance from one key to the very next, up or down, black or white

interval .... the distance between two notes or keys

legato .... to play smooth and connected

major .... follows the **W W H W** pattern in a pentascale

minor .... follows the **W H W W** pattern in a pentascale

mezzo forte .... moderately loud (mf)

mezzo piano .... moderately soft (mp)

natural .... the symbol that cancels a sharp or flat ($\natural$)

parallel motion .... both parts move in the same direction while remaining the same distance apart

pentascale .... a 5-note pattern of whole and half steps

piano .... soft (p)

repeat sign .... the symbol indicating that the previous section is to be repeated ($:\|$)

sharp .... the symbol that raises a note a half step ($\sharp$)

root .... the note on which a triad is built

staccato .... to play detached by releasing the key quickly

transpose .... to play exactly the same pattern of notes, starting on a different key

triad .... a three-note chord

whole step .... two half steps, or twice the distance of a half step

PENTASCALE AND TRIAD GLOSSARY

Now you can test your skill by filling in all the accidentals that are necessary on this page.

FF1